Bruce Brooks Pfeiffer

FRANK LLOYD WRIGHT

1867 – 1959

Building for Democracy

TASCHEN

KÖLN LONDON LOS ANGELES MADRID PARIS TOKYO

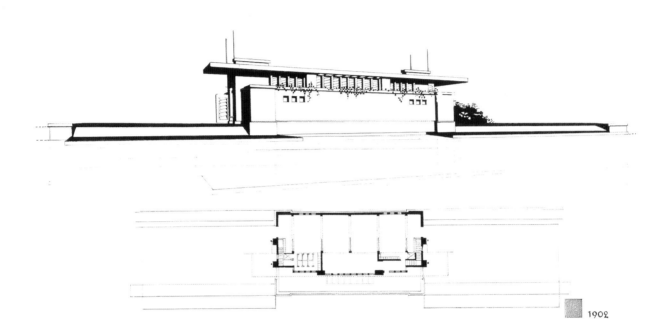

1902

Image page 2 ► Frank Lloyd Wright standing at
the drawing table
Illustration page 4 ► Yahara River Boat House,
Madison, Wisconsin, 1905, perspective and plan

The drawings of Frank Lloyd Wright are Copyright
© The Frank Lloyd Wright Foundation, Scottsdale,
Arizona, 2004

© 2004 TASCHEN GmbH
Hohenzollernring 53, D-50672 Köln
www.taschen.com

Edited by ► Peter Gössel
Project management ► Katrin Schumann
Design and layout ► Gössel und Partner

Printed in Germany
ISBN 3-8228-2757-6

Contents

Introduction

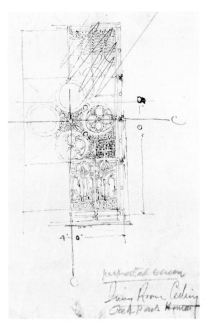

Perforated screen, dining room ceiling in the Frank Lloyd Wright House, Oak Park, Illinois, 1889
Wright maintained that this dining room lighting fixture was the first example of indirect lighting.

Opposite page:
Library in the Frank Lloyd Wright Studio, Oak Park, Illinois, 1897
It was here that Wright showed his clients their drawings, the room being well lit by both daylight and incandescent fixtures.

In 1895, Nathan G. Moore, a prominent Chicago attorney and Oak Park neighbor of architect Frank Lloyd Wright, came into Wright's Schiller Building office and asked him to design a house. He had one important stipulation: "Now we want you to build our house, but I don't want you to give us anything like that house you did for Winslow. I don't want to go down the backstreets to my morning train to avoid being laughed at."[1] To understand the sensation made by that one home, tucked quietly away in a sedate, wooded suburb, we must consider the architecture in the United States at that time; and in particular, the architecture of Chicago and its environs.

The architecture of the United States at the turn of the century – 1895 to 1905 – was, at best, a collection of eclectic styles, with hardly one relating in any way or sense to the ideal of the nation in which it was built. This was an era which regarded architecture as an application of fashions and styles, unrelated to structure or construction techniques. Yet it was also a time when the entire construction industry was undergoing revolutionary changes. New materials were emerging, and new methods of handling the older materials were being developed at the same time. But the architecture being designed reflected little if anything of those new methods and materials.

The Chicago Fair of 1893, the Columbian Exposition, was a supreme case in point. On the one hand, Louis Sullivan claimed that the Exposition "put American architecture behind for at least 50 years"[2]; while on the other hand, Daniel Burnham, a fashionable Chicago architect of the time, lauded the fair as an example of what the Americans would want to build. He told Wright, when urging him to go to the Beaux-Arts in Paris, "The Fair, Frank, is going to have a great influence in our country. The American people have seen the Classics on a grand scale for the first time."[3]

The young architect, just starting his own practice with the William H. Winslow house (and Burnham said of that work: "A gentleman's home, from grade to coping.") replied, "No, there is Louis Sullivan ... And if John Root were alive I don't believe he would feel that way about it. Richardson I am sure never would." Burnham further argued, "Frank, the Fair should have shown you that Sullivan and Richardson are well enough in their way, but their way won't prevail – architecture is going the other way."[4] And of course, it was. It is ironical to realize that the date of that architectural disaster of 1893 coincides with the date at which Frank Lloyd Wright opened his private architectural practice, after nearly seven years spent in the office of Adler and Sullivan, in Chicago.

Richardson, Sullivan, and Wright. The progression of these three architects has been cited over and over again as the progression of an American architecture from classicism towards a new ideal. Richardson was certainly steeped in a Romanesque tradition, but his work still bears a remarkably masculine, truly American, virility and strength of its own. Sullivan, the poet, the designing partner of the Chicago firm Adler and Sullivan, made the tall building truly tall, not just piling up massive masonry boxes. In his work, the tall, long, accentuated vertical line gave birth to the true aesthetic expression of the skyscraper.

Both Richardson and Sullivan were educated, urbane and highly sophisticated. Both attended school on the East coast, both went to Paris to the École des Beaux-Arts. None of this was the case with Wright. His background, by contrast, was steeped in strong Unitarian, transcendental principles. He was raised in a rather poor family, his father a minister and music teacher, his mother a teacher. He spent his younger boyhood on his uncle's farm in southwestern Wisconsin. His surroundings were pastoral, educational, agricultural, and strongly Welsh. On his mother's side he was descended from ministers, farmers, and educators, who came to the New World in 1844 from Wales. He grew up in their ancestral valley, and it was to that valley that he returned, after leaving wife and family behind in Oak Park, to build his own home, Taliesin, at the age of 44.

Combined with this ancestral background and through the influence of his mother he was brought up on the writings and teachings of such Americans as Whitman, Thoreau and Emerson, combined with Byron, Shelley and Blake. He soon learned to read and absorb Schiller and Goethe; on the trolley to school he carried a pocket version of Shakespeare's plays and sonnets. He was steeped in music, especially Bach and Beethoven, due to the daily influence of his father, who played Bach chorales on the organ in church (the young Frank confined to pumping the bellows) and in the evening Beethoven sonatas on the piano at home. "I fell asleep night after night to strains of Beethoven sonatas all throughout my early childhood," Wright admitted.

Now, at the same time that he was immersed in these influences of literature, poetry, philosophy, and music, he was also right in the middle of the Industrial Revolution. This should have fostered in him irreconcilable conflicts both in purpose and in ethics, but it did not. In fact, it was this combination that made him the person he was and the architect he became. The Industrial Revolution gave him the tools he needed to build the buildings his fertile imagination created; the transcendental background posited in him an abiding sense of human values. Here we have a striking paradox: industrial tools and methods, human values and a deep love for nature. Both elements were essential to his work; he could not envision the one without the other.

He claimed that it was his mother who determined his profession, that while carrying him, she determined that the child she was to bear would be a son, who would grow to be a great architect. She nurtured his early childhood based on that conviction. She surrounded him with natural beauty, she discovered the Kindergarten Gifts of Friedrich Froebel and brought them home to her son. He took to the Gifts with a passion. When his mother realized that drawing and designing were becoming his one consuming interest, she believed it was time to introduce another, counterbalancing, factor in his early training. Consulting with her brother James Lloyd Jones, a farmer living in the family valley nearby, it was decided to send the boy to work on the farm during the summers.

A great part of his own autobiography is concerned, in the story of his early years, not with his education in school, but his education at work on the farm.

Those boyhood experiences had rooted deeply values and memories of so strong a nature, sometimes so heartbreaking and backbreaking, that his own recollection, 54 years later, prompted him to regard those years as his most formative.

Hardly off the farm and past his boyhood years, he enrolled as a special student in the University of Wisconsin School of Engineering, but grew dissatisfied and after a short term ran away to Chicago to pursue a life in architecture. But before leaving

James Charnley House, Chicago, Illinois, 1891
"In this Charnley city-house on Astor Street I first sensed the definitively decorative value of the plain surface, that is to say, of the flat plane as such. The drawings for the Charnley house were all traced and printed in the Adler and Sullivan offices, but by preparing them for this purpose at home I helped pay my pressing building debts with 'overtime.' "

Madison, Wisconsin, he witnessed the collapse of the new north wing of the old State Capitol building, then in construction. The contractor saw no fault in filling the cores of the new massive hollow piers with broken bricks and stones during construction, and the added weight proved too much: the piers gave way one summer afternoon and the structure collapsed. Workmen trapped in the building were crushed to death as floors collapsed and pinned them in. Throughout the afternoon and evening rescuers dug bodies of wounded, dying and dead out of the debris. Standing nearby was the young Wright. "The youth stayed for hours, clinging to the iron fence that surrounded the park, too heartsick to move – to go away. The horror of that scene has never entirely left his consciousness and remains to prompt him to this day,"[5] he wrote. In Chicago, after taking jobs at other architectural firms, Wright was encouraged to try for a job with Louis Sullivan, engaged at that time with the design of the Chicago Auditorium, and desperately in need of designers to assist him. With Adler and Sullivan for nearly seven years, Wright quit, following a heated disagreement with Sullivan over the terms of his contract (he was building "boot-leg" houses on his own time). He set up his own practice in the Schiller Building, built by Adler and Sullivan, and into his office came his first client, William H. Winslow, of River Forest, Illinois.

The "prairie house" has come to mean, in recent years, a certain type of residential design employed by Wright during the years 1900 to 1911. Wright himself did not use the term "prairie house," rather he spoke and wrote of the type of dwelling he thought most appropriate to the Midwest prairie around Chicago and its suburbs. "We of the Middle West," he wrote in the March 1908 issue of Architectural Record, "are living on the prairie. The prairie has a beauty of its own and we should recognize and accentuate this natural beauty, its quiet level. Hence, gently sloping roofs, low proportions, quiet sky lines, suppressed heavy-set chimneys, and sheltering overhangs, low terraces and out-reaching walls sequestering private gardens." And later in An Autobiography, first published in 1932, he revealed, "I loved the prairie by instinct as great simplicity – the trees, the flowers, the sky itself, thrilling by contrast. I saw that a little of height on the prairie was enough to look like much more – every detail as to height becoming intensely

Ornamental Details for Chicago Auditorium, 1888
Wright assisted Sullivan in the development of the interior designs for the Chicago Auditorium. On this drawing Wright later inscribed, "Fragment of bronze newel-post head – Auditorium Chicago." The other portion of this fragment is located in the Avery Architectural and Fine Arts Library at Columbia University in New York.

Frank Thomas House, Oak Park, Illinois, 1901
"Making away with the box both in plan and elevation now became fundamental to my work. That opened the way for feeling the space within as the Reality of all true modern building, building not merely monumental. I have sought this liberation in some form or other in almost every building I have built."

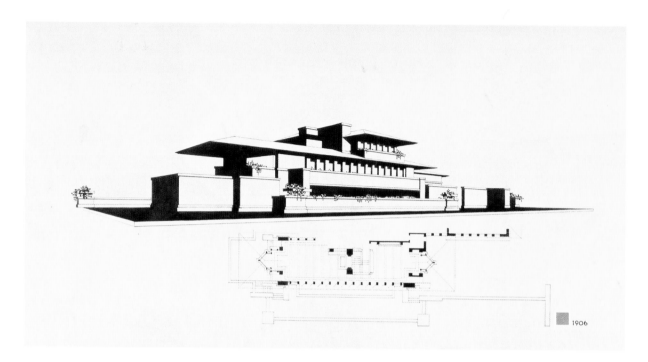

1906

significant, breadths all falling short ... I had an idea that the horizontal planes in buildings belong to the ground. I began putting this idea to work."[6]

That quality of the broad, extended horizontal line, the low proportions associated closely with the ground, the broad overhangs and gently sloping roofs are the distinctive features which characterize his early domestic architecture. But behind those exterior features a whole new language of architecture was being born. It did not happen overnight, and following the Winslow house of 1893 it took almost seven years for the ideas and forms to evolve.

The first step in this direction developed quite naturally in the plan of the home: more open spaces, screened off from one another by simple architectural devices rather than partitions and doors. This eventually came to be known as the "open plan." The integration of the building with its natural site was another development. Those earlier houses were in suburbs, when suburbs were sparsely populated, the landscaping equally sparse. Wright believed that on this flat, extended prairie it was desirable to get up off the ground to provide a wider outlook. For that reason he raised the basement floor to ground level, letting it serve as a pedestal for the main floor above. In elevation he began to see the walls of the house more as screens, the walls rising directly from the base or water table, the second story windows a continuous band beneath the eaves. The cement stucco of the extended eaves was painted a light color, which brought reflected light into rooms that would otherwise have been dark. The open-swinging window, as opposed to the double hung or "guillotine" window let more air into the rooms, the window openings were protected against sun and wind by the overhanging eaves. In this use of materials, he advised the application of a mono-material rather than the conglomerate fashionable at the time. Cement stucco houses were cement stucco throughout, accented by wood trim. The same applied to brick masonry. If there was a combination of materials, such as brick and stucco, it

Frederick C. Robie House, Chicago, Illinois, 1908, perspective and plan
Wright once remarked, "Give me an enlightened businessman and I can change the face of the nation." In Frederick Robie, Wright did indeed find such a person, and his house played a most significant role in changing the face of American domestic architecture.

was kept consistent throughout the elevation of the building, all in an attempt to achieve repose and simplicity.

The handling and developing of all these elements expanded and grew from the early houses such as Bradley, Dana and Willits to the later ones, such as Martin, Coonley and Robie. But from first to last, they were all conceived as homes for the prairie, and although they fall into different design types, this one common denominator – the Midwest prairie – groups them together despite their individual differences.

All along, in the "prairie houses," Wright's concept of interior space was becoming more and more the significant feature of the building. It grew slowly, and he pointed out the living room of the Hillside Home School, 1902, as a significant step in that direction. The four large stone columns that carry the balcony around the living room are placed in from the window edge, the balcony itself is also in from the tall windows that run unimpeded from sill to soffit above. In this Hillside living room it is evident that the window walls are non-supporting screens, supports for the structure being placed in from the edge. The designs for the Larkin Building, in Buffalo, New York, and Unity Temple, in Oak Park, Illinois, soon followed. While Wright was at work on the Larkin commission, a plaster model of the building was made and delivered to his Oak Park Studio. He recalled, "Suddenly, the model was standing on the studio table in the center. I came in and saw what was the matter. I took those four corners and I pulled them away from the building, made them individual features, planted them. And there began the thing that I was trying to do ... I got features instead of walls. I followed that up with Unity Temple where there were no walls of any kind, only features, and the features were screens grouped about interior space. The thing that had come to me by instinct in the Larkin Building began to come consciously in Unity Temple. When I finished Unity Temple, I had it. I was conscious of the idea. I knew I had the beginning of a great thing, a great truth in architecture. And now architecture could be free."[7]

What he had achieved in Unity Temple was, in his own words, the "destruction of the box" in architecture. Exterior walls were no longer the support of the overhead, be it slab or sloped roof. Cantilever construction placed the supports in from the outside edge, much like the extended arm of the branches of a tree. The walls outside now became non-supporting elements which he termed "screens," either opaque – concrete, masonry or wood –, or transparent – glass windows and glass doors. The interior space took on a new freedom and at the same time a closer relationship to the landscape of nature outside. That once so limited distinction between exterior and interior vanished, and a new flow from one to the other became possible and wholly desirable. All of this act, this freeing of the interior to the exterior, gave meaning to the phrase "the space within became the reality of the building," not the walls or ceilings.

In his very first work, Frank Lloyd Wright manifested a careful knowledge and diligent respect for natural materials. He saw the general lack of such respect in the work of other architects of his era, as well as previous eras. Stone, brick and wood – those basic architectural materials – had long been covered, painted, plastered, and altered to suit any particular fashion or taste. His work in these materials always adhered to what he perceived as most natural to them, letting the masses of stone become the feature of the building, or the rich earth-tones of the brick, product of the kiln, rise in masses and forms that glorified the brick. And wood he considered the most loved of all materials, saying "Wood is universally beautiful to man. Man loves his association with it; likes to feel it under his hand, sympathetic to his touch and to his eye."[8]

Thomas P. Hardy House, Racine, Wisconsin, 1905, perspective

11

Not only were the natural materials ignored in most nineteenth century architecture, but even the newer materials, concrete, steel, sheet metal and glass, were used in outdated ways. He perceived these new materials and the methods of using them as a wonderful "tool box" for the architect of the twentieth century. Steel combined with concrete – reinforced concrete – was the great liberating element that could produce an entirely new architecture for the twentieth century. The Johnson Wax building, Kaufmann's Fallingwater, the Johnson Wax Research Tower and Price Tower, and the Guggenheim Museum are all examples of the use of reinforced concrete cantilever construction.

Realizing early on in the twentieth century that handicraft work was becoming more and more costly, thus less and less desirable for general architectural design, Frank Lloyd Wright turned to the machine and machine methods. The idea of prefabrication in housing appealed to him as well, and in 1915 he began work along that line in the American Ready Cut System Houses. But the concept and the scheme proved too far in advance of what industry, housing, and construction financing would permit at that time. The four concrete block houses in Los Angeles are a splendid example of what Wright meant when he said the "machine should be a tool in the hand of the artist." In this case, the "machine" was the form, or mold, into which the concrete was poured in order to form the block. Up until this time concrete block was the "gutter-child" of the building trade. Wright saw that the block, if treated as a decorative as well as structural element, could rise into the air and sunlight as a beautiful product.

Other facets of the building industry he treated the same way: sheet metal, too, could be turned by machine from simple, unadorned sheets of steel, copper, and aluminum into patterned surfaces to adorn the edifice.

Like all the transcendentalists, Frank Lloyd Wright regarded nature in almost mystical terms. He deeply believed that the closer man associated himself with nature, the greater his personal, spiritual and even physical well-being grew and expanded as a direct result of that association. Wright liked to refer to his way of thinking of nature as "Nature spelled with a capital 'N' the way you spell God with a capital 'G,' " and he further maintained that "Nature is all the body of God we will ever know."[9]

From this point of view, from his reverence and subsequently his respect for nature, his buildings, where placed in the landscape, had this one aim in common: to let the human being experience and participate in the joys and wonderment of natural beauty. Today we call it site planning, environmental design and all manner of sophisticated terms that really mean the same thing: respect for the earth. Without that respect the earth, as we know it, is destined to become a dead planet, covered by an equally dead sky. Civilization today is faced with that perilous fear and now for the first time begins to take grasp of the fear and act as a result of that fear. Nearly 100 years ago, Wright offered solutions in the form of architecture, showing how to live in harmony with the environment, not out of fear (a mere animal instinct, basically) but out of a deeply-rooted love for natural beauty. It was his conviction that mankind, if exposed to and set into the fabric of Nature, would respond affirmatively and grow spiritually.

His eloquence in the manner in which he wrote and spoke of nature is surpassed only by the buildings he set on earth.

With these aforementioned ideas and principles – interior space, thus exterior form, materials and methods, nature and environment – at his disposal like pencils in

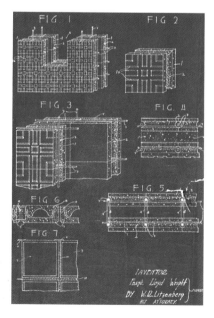

Concrete Block Diagrams for Patent Application, circa 1923

his hand, Frank Lloyd Wright continued to draw the designs and buildings that would change the face of architecture in the world. He elected to call his buildings "organic architecture," a phrase that was initiated by his "Lieber Meister," Louis Sullivan. But he went far beyond Sullivan in his work and in his interpretation of that definition. Wright sometimes referred to organic architecture as one in which all the parts were related to the whole, as the whole was related to the parts: continuity and integrity. But in an even broader, and deeper sense, he said that an organic building, wherever it stood in time, was appropriate to time, appropriate to place, and appropriate to man. Using that lexicon as a guideline, one can trace all the great buildings down through all the great epochs of time, and conversely one can eliminate a great many other ventures into the art of architecture as mere fashion or sham.

Wright's work progressed as his own ever-creative mind expanded. From the massive, sculptural office building for the Larkin Company, he made, 30 years later, the fluid, plastic, curvilinear, light, and airy office building for the S. C. Johnson & Son Company. From the formal "sphinx-like" plan of the Imperial Hotel and Midway Gardens, evolved the ultimate concept of a fluid space flow, again 30 years later, in the Guggenheim Museum. From the simple house of Mrs. Thomas Gale on a simple lot on the Midwest prairie, Oak Park, 1909, he progressed to the concrete and stone terraces projecting out and over a waterfall in a wooded glen in Western Pennsylvania, the world-famous house for Edgar J. Kaufmann, Fallingwater. From the windmill tower Romeo and Juliet, a wooden tower set on a stone base reinforced with iron rods, sixty

Frank Lloyd Wright with Guggenheim Model at *Sixty Years of Living Architecture* exhibition, New York, 1953
This was the largest exhibition of Wright's work ever mounted. After opening in Philadelphia in 1951, the show traveled widely in Europe, then went on to Mexico City before returning to the States in 1953 with venues in New York and Los Angeles. In New York, it was shown in this special pavilion built on the site of the future Guggenheim Museum.

years passed until the opening of the Price Tower, in Bartlesville, Oklahoma, in 1956. From the square-formed, monolithic, sculptural beauty of Unity Temple, where light poured in from the clerestory and ceiling above, evolved the design, almost half a century later, of the Beth Sholom Synagogue, a building that seems fabricated, embraced by, and enveloped in Light.

The forms in each of these examples are different, but the principles are consistent. It was the strict adherence to, and belief in the validity of principle that was the guiding force in all Wright's work.

From beginning to end, throughout all the work of Frank Lloyd Wright, one important element remains constant, prevails over all other considerations, remains, in fact, always the first consideration: human values. He often called it "Humanity." From simple dwelling place to vast civic center, from factory to cathedral, from farm to school, wherever man is placed in relation to Wright's buildings, man is placed ostensibly in the center.

Nearing the end of his life, Wright wrote a book in 1957 called *A Testament*. It is part biographical and part explanatory, reviewing his work, how it came about, the significant principles, works and results. He summed up the forces that made his work, as he saw them, and the forms of all great Art, likewise as he saw them. In the last chapter of the book he wrote a chapter entitled "Humanity – The Light of the World," part of which is included here: "Constantly I have referred to a more 'humane' architecture, so I will try to explain what humane means to me, an architect. Like organic architecture,

Christmas Eve concert at Taliesin II, December 24, 1924

In attendance, from left to right: Frank Lloyd Wright, Richard Neutra, Sylva Moser with baby Lorenz, Kameki Tsuchiura, Nobu Tsuchiura, Werner Moser, and Dione Neutra.

the quality of humanity is interior to man. As the solar system is reckoned in terms of light-years, so may the inner light be what we are calling humanity. This element, Man as light, is beyond all reckoning. Buddha was known as the light of Asia; Jesus as the light of the world. Sunlight is to nature as this interior light is to man's spirit: Manlight.

Manlight is above instinct. Human imagination by way of this interior light is born, conceives, creates: dies but to continue the light of existence only as this light lived in the man. The spirit is illumined by it and to the extent that his life is this light and it proceeds from him, it in turn illumines his kind. Affirmations of this light in human life and work are man's true happiness.

There is nothing higher in human consciousness than beams of this interior light. We call them beauty. Beauty is but the shining of man's light – radiance the high romance of his manhood as we know Architecture, the Arts, Philosophy, Religion, to be romantic. All come to nourish or be nourished by this inextinguishable light within the soul of man. He can give no intellectual consideration above or beyond this inspiration. From the cradle to the grave his true being craves this reality to assure the continuation of his life as Light thereafter.

As sunlight falls around a helpless thing, revealing form and countenance, so a corresponding light, of which the sun is a symbol, shines from the inspired work of mankind. This inner light is assurance that man's Architecture, Art and Religion, are as one – its symbolic emblems. Then we may call humanity itself the light that never fails. Baser elements in man are subject to this miracle of his own light. Sunrise and sunset are appropriate symbols of Man's existence on earth.

There is no more precious element of immortality than mankind as thus humane. Heaven may be the symbol of this light of lights only insofar as heaven is thus a haven."[10]

1   *An Autobiography*, Frank Lloyd Wright, Longmans, Green, NY, 1932
2   *A Testament*, Frank Lloyd Wright, New York, NY, 1957, p. 57
3   Ibid., p. 124
4   Ibid., p. 124
5   Ibid.
6   Ibid.
7   Talk to the Taliesin Fellowship, August 13, 1952
8   *Architectural Record*, May, 1928
9   Mike Wallace Interview, September, 1957
10 *A Testament*, Frank Lloyd Wright, New York, NY, 1957

1893–1894 · William H. Winslow House
River Forest, Illinois

Perspective

"Uncle Dan [Daniel H. Burnham] had seen the Winslow house and straightway pronounced it 'a gentleman's house from grade to coping.' ... The Winslow house had burst on the view of that provincial suburb like the Prima Vera in fullbloom. It was a new world to Oak Park and River Forest. That house became an attraction, far and near. Incessantly it was courted and admired."

By today's standards the house for William H. Winslow is simple, noble and elegant, but in 1894 was so unusual that it was the subject of neighborly ridicule. A number of features in this house are a marked departure from standards customary in 19th century residential architecture in the Midwest. The walls rise directly from a cast stone coping – which Wright termed "water-table" – and use a minimum amount of planting around the base of the building to emphasize the union of house and earth. Instead of the steeply pitched roofs pierced by tall, slim chimneys, the roof slopes gently down from a large, generous chimney mass and projects out and over the second story windows. The windows themselves rise from sill to soffit, rather than stopping a foot or so below, and thus become openings in a screen, rather than holes in a wall. The materials are treated in a manner consistent with the nature and color of each: cast concrete

First floor plan

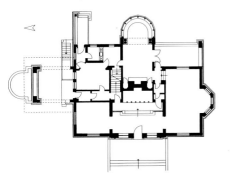

is left pure, pristine white; golden Roman brick is golden Roman brick; the terracotta frieze on the second story wall surface is deep brown terracotta. This was in an era when brick was plastered, wood was painted, concrete was covered, etc. Inside, the spaces are clearly defined, but flow from one to another on the ground floor, instead of being the customary collection of boxes within boxes. The woodwork is clean, simple, and natural, a minimum of tooling and lathing replacing overwrought carving and curlicues common at the time. The whole has an understated elegant dignity previously unknown in that era of overstatement.

1900 · "A Home in a Prairie Town"

for "Ladies' Home Journal" (project)

Perspective drawing

"My sense of 'wall' was no longer the side of a box. It was enclosure of space affording protection against storm or heat only when needed. But it was also to bring the outside world into the house and let the inside of the house go outside."

When "A Home in a Prairie Town" was published in 1901 in "Ladies' Home Journal," Wright supplied not only the drawings for the house but the text as well. It puts on record some of his earliest writing concerning the "prairie house": "The exterior recognizes the influence of the prairie, is firmly and broadly associated with the site, and makes a feature of its quiet level. The low terraces and broad eaves are designed to accentuate that quiet level and complete the harmonious relationship." In conjunction with the plans, sections and views of this house is a suggestion for its use as part of a quadruple block in which four such houses are grouped towards the center each one facing its own corner, with privacy from the others.

1901–1902 ▸ William G. Fricke House
Oak Park, Illinois

Street view

Below:
Plan, first floor
The pavilion was later demolished.

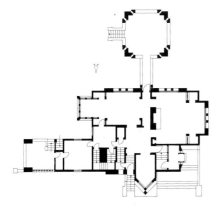

The William G. Fricke house is a special example of a three-story house designed by Frank Lloyd Wright. The size of the lot imposed on the architect the need to go up, rather than out. The placement of the house on the lot demonstrates an important design solution: the house is set to one corner, freeing the rest for lawn and gardens, defying standards which placed the house in the center, with yards in front, at the back and on either side. Originally, a roofed-over but open pavilion was reached by a covered passage from the living room. Ideal for summer entertaining and dining, the pavilion was set in the shade, overlooking flowering gardens.

1902–1903 ▸ Ward W. Willits House
Highland Park, Illinois

Above:
Street view

Opposite page:
Dining room with original furniture

Below:
Plan, first floor

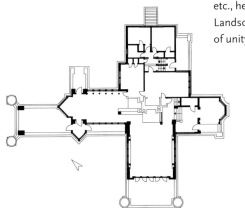

On a more spacious suburban lot is the house of Ward W. Willits. Built of cement stucco, its white surfaces are accentuated by dark stained wood trim. The plan is cruciform, the living room, dining room and reception areas separated by architectural features rather than walls and doors. As with the Dana house, the fireplace is focal to the plan, with built-in seats around it. More and more, in his early work, Wright experimented with furniture of his own design. He found, to his dismay, that when the new house was ready for the clients to move in, they brought with them the furniture of their previous dwelling. By incorporating built-in bookcases, seating, sideboards, cupboards, etc., he was certain that the basic interior, at least, would blend with his overall design. Landscaping, as well, was designed along with the building to further achieve a sense of unity in design.

1903–1905 · Larkin Building
Company Administration Building ▸ Buffalo, New York

Interior, side gallery

Opposite page:
Street view

More than any other single structure in the twentieth century, the Larkin Building exerted an influence that changed the face of architecture. "The building," Wright wrote, "is a simple working out of certain utilitarian conditions, its exterior a simple cliff of brick whose only 'ornamental' feature is the exterior expression of the central aisle, fashioned by means of the sculptured piers at either end of the main block. The machinery of the various appurtenance systems, pipe shafts incidental thereto, the heating and ventilating air intakes, and the stairways which serve also as fire escapes, are quartered in plan and placed outside the main building at the four outer corners, so that the entire area might be free for working purposes. These stair chambers are toplighted. The interior of the main building thus forms a single large room in which the main

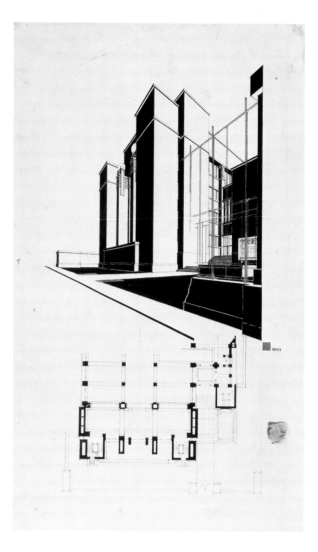

Perspective and partial plan

Varnished metal office chair
Frank Lloyd Wright drew numerous models for his
furniture. This office chair with wheels came in
another version as well, which hung from the
table. This was intended to make cleaning the
room easier.

floors are galleries open to a large central court, which is also lighted from above. All the windows of the various stories 'galleries' are seven feet above the floor, the space beneath being utilized for steel filing cabinets. The window sashes are double, and the building practically sealed to dirt, odor and noise, fresh air being taken high above the ground in shafts extending above the roof surfaces."

There were many innovative details of the building that marked it an important "first of its kind": steel desk furniture, air-conditioning, wall-hung water closet and partitions (for ease in cleaning), glass doors set in metal frames with pintle hinges (anchored at top and bottom). The general disposition of the entire plan, working in open galleries looking into a light court, brought a sense of "family" to the corporation where all worked together without private offices or secluded spaces. This in itself was a great revolution in industrial thought in an era where the employer was usually sequestered from the employee.

Above left:
A special feature of this building was the multilevel court with a glass roof, which served as an open-plan office.

Above right:
Reception desk in the work area, third floor

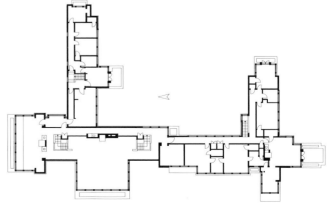

1907–1908 · Avery Coonley House
Riverside, Illinois

Living room
The rugs and furniture were all designed by Wright with ceiling grilles for indirect lighting. The wall mural is by George Niedecken.

Opposite page above:
View from pool

Opposite page below:
Plan, main level

When Avery and Queene Ferry Coonley came into Wright's office and asked him to design their home the architect asked what prompted them to choose him. Mrs. Coonley replied that as they saw his other houses they saw in his work "the countenances of principle." Writing about that commission, he said, "This was to me a great and sincere compliment. So I put my best into the Coonley House." The Coonleys had ample space on a wooded flat lot in which to place a house that could spread out. The plan was one that Wright called "zoned" because of the separation of the different functions: living, dining in one wing, bedrooms stretching out in another, and a third for kitchen and servants, crossing over the entrance drive and reaching into gardens beyond.

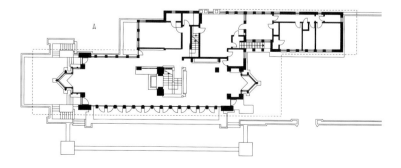

1908–1909 · Frederick C. Robie House
Chicago, Illinois

Dining room

One of the reasons the house for Frederick C. Robie was such a successful work were the explicit requirements on the part of the client. He wanted a house that was fire-proof, that did not have boxed up spaces, that had none of the usual "decorator" items such as draperies, store bought carpets, etc. He was an engineer by training and de-sired a home that worked as well as any fine machine. The corner lot location of the Robie house explains many of its design factors: the ground floor, like so many of the prairie houses, contains playroom, billiard room, heating, laundry, and storage. Access to the house is on this level, set on the side of the plan, with stairs to the main floor. This is basically one long space, with a fireplace in the center, which divides the living room at one end from the dining room at the other. On the third level are the bedrooms, rising in their own tower-like belvedere.

The furniture for the house was all designed by Wright; the dining room table and chairs are especially famous. The table places four stands at the four corners, contain-ing stained glass lamps and shelves for flower arrangements. There was a definite idea behind this design: most flower arrangements, with candlesticks and candles, run down the center of the table as a visual barrier between host, hostess and guests. Here, however, all decoration and lighting is safely placed at the corners to let the cen-ter remain free and open.

Living room

Opposite page above:
Street view

Opposite page below:
Plan, first floor

1909 ‣ Mrs. Thomas Gale House
Oak Park, Illinois

Perspective drawing

For a house as small as the house for Mrs. Thomas Gale, the elevation is strikingly modern with the projecting balconies and flat roof overhangs. Wright referred to the house as "the progenitor of Fallingwater," and it is obvious how he made the association of the two. The living room and dining room of the house are not raised above ground, as was being done rather consistently with other prairie houses, and it has a full basement. The living room opens directly onto a low walled terrace, or porch. The lot is an unusually small one, which accounts for the compactness of the plan.

1912–1913 · Avery Coonley Playhouse
Riverside, Illinois

Street view

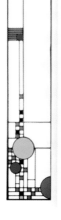

Stained glass window
The designs for the Coonley Playhouse windows possess such charm and delight that they form the patterns for various products today that range from textiles to glassware as approved by the Frank Lloyd Wright Foundation in its licensing program.

Avery and Queene Ferry Coonley were intensely concerned with education. The special school and playhouse was the answer. The straight-line, streamline-masses, flatroof overhangs, perforated trellises and general design composition predate such works as Midway Gardens, the Emil Bach house, and the Imperial Hotel. An especially delightful feature of the playhouse are the brightly colored windows, called "Balloons and Confetti."

1911–1959 · Taliesin
Frank Lloyd Wright House, Studio and Farm
▸ Spring Green, Wisconsin

Opposite page:
Blue Loggia, Taliesin III, 1925

Living room, Taliesin II, 1915

The word "Taliesin" is Welsh for "shining brow," and Wright chose it as the name for his home in southwestern Wisconsin for two reasons: his Welsh ancestry and the placement of the house on the brow of the hill. The low one-story structure was wrapped around the brow of the hill with spectacular views over the lake below and surrounding hills. The other side of the long L-shaped house and studio opened onto secluded garden courts. Twice destroyed by fire, the building that stands today, Taliesin III, is a much larger, more expansive structure, which still preserves the harmonious relationship to the hillside, the garden courts and hill crown.

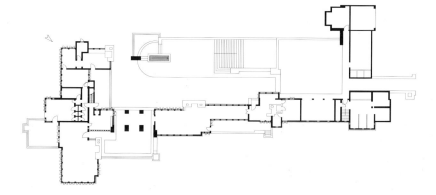

Plan, Taliesin I

1912–1914 · Francis W. Little House

"Northome" ▸ Wayzata, Minnesota

In 1900 Wright designed and built a home for Francis W. Little in Peoria, Illinois. In 1908, the Littles requested designs for a summer home on the shores of Lake Minnetonka, near Minneapolis, which never went beyond preliminary planning. In 1911/12, the Littles asked Wright to design a more substantial residence, but his travels to Europe and Japan intervened, and it was not until 1913 that a scheme was finally ready. The house stretched across a low hill facing the lake. A rather monumental flight of concrete steps bordered by low brick walls ascended to the main level, which contained living room, library and bedrooms. A lower level contained a dining room with a terrace bordering the lake, a kitchen and an additional bedroom for guests. The house was demolished in 1972, but the main rooms and art glass were saved. The living room is located now in New York's Metropolitan Museum of Art, the library in Pennsylvania's Allentown Museum.

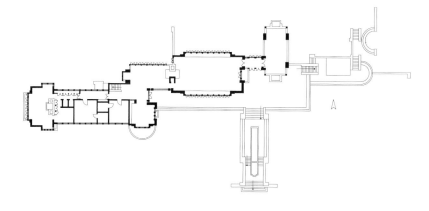

Plan, main level

Left:

Installation of the living room at the Metropolitan Museum of Art, New York
The wood strips are typical of Wright's use of "back band" to add integral architectural features on the ceiling and down to the clerestory windows. The statue, "Victory of Samothrace," was a reproduction much admired by Wright and was chosen specifically for several of his clients' residences.

1915–1922 · Imperial Hotel
Tokyo, Japan

A supreme example of the use of reinforced concrete is the Imperial Hotel in Tokyo. In this building two considerations were paramount: a structure that would withstand earthquakes and be fireproof against the infernos that inevitably follow. For this to be a fireproof structure the traditional wood and paper architecture of Japan had to give way to reinforced concrete, stone and brick. To render the building capable of surviving earthquakes, Wright developed a system of foundations and structural support hitherto unseen in architecture. The principle at work was the cantilever, the balanced load, not unlike the tray held overhead on the outstretched hand of a waiter. In place of heavy tile roofs of traditional Japanese architecture, the roof of the Imperial Hotel was made of thin copper plates. The whole structure rode on a network of thin concrete pins, nine feet deep and two feet apart throughout, that connected the building above to a mud substrata below. Flexibility, by means of reinforced concrete, was the principle which saved the building in the Kanto Quake of 1923.

View over dining room to Peacock Room

Opposite page:
The Promenade

1917–1920 ▸ Aline Barnsdall House

"Hollyhock House" ▸ Los Angeles, California

By 1922, Wright had returned from Japan, the hotel nearly completed, and had established himself in Los Angeles to continue with work for Aline Barnsdall. Her love was drama and she had purchased a substantial piece of property in the heart of Los Angeles called Olive Hill. At the hill's base, she planned a large theater, motion picture theater, residences for actors and directors, and a series of shops and stores. On the hill above was to be her own home, Hollyhock House. None of her theater plans were carried out, but her own house and two others, called "Residence A" and "Residence B," were built. The house was designed with the south-west climate in mind: walls facing the hot California sun have a minimum of exposed glass, while generous areas of glass doors open into a central, cool green patio.

Right:
Living room

Below:
Plan

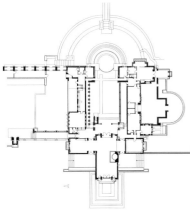

Opposite page:
Front elevation

1923–1924 › Alice Millard House

"La Miniatura" › Pasadena, California

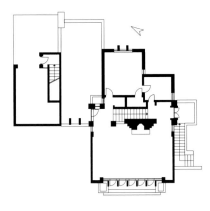

In general, Wright's work is predominantly horizontal: certainly the great majority of the prairie houses were such, and some of the larger non-residential work, such as Midway Gardens and the Imperial Hotel bear this distinctive characteristic. With the prairie it was his intention to accentuate the long, low horizontal line, and in the Midway Gardens and Imperial Hotel that same emphasis prevailed. But here, in a narrow ravine in Pasadena, is a work that has strongly vertical elements and vertical significance. The house for Alice Millard was the first house to be built of the new system he had innovated and named "textile block construction." "We would take that despised outcast of the building industry – the concrete block ... find hitherto unsuspected soul in it – make it live as a thing of beauty – textured like the trees. All we would have to do would be to educate the concrete block, refine it and knit it together with steel in the joints ... The walls would thus become thin but solid reinforced slabs and yield to any desire for form imaginable."

Above:
Plan

Right:
Living room
Alice Millard was a dealer in rare books, paintings, prints, and antiques. Her home was also her gallery.

Opposite page:
View at entrance

1929 ▸ "Ocatillo"

Frank Lloyd Wright Desert Compound ▸ near Chandler, Arizona

Partial view

"I presently found that the white luminous canvas overhead and canvas used instead of window glass afforded such agreeable diffusion of light within, was so enjoyable and sympathetic to the desert that I now felt more than ever oppressed by the thought of the opaque solid overhead of the much too heavy mid-western house ... So 'Ocatillo' – our little desert camp – you are 'ephemera,' nevertheless you will drop a seed or two yourself in course of time." Those seeds, of course, grew to become Taliesin West a decade later.

When Wright was called to Chandler, Arizona, to design the resort hotel San Marcos-in-the-Desert, the client, Dr. Alexander Chandler, presented him with two options: rent space in town for his family and draftsmen, or build something out on the desert not far from the site of the projected new hotel. Wright naturally chose to build, and Chandler let him have his pick of any site in the region. The desert encampment, called Ocatillo after the desert cactus in the region, was his first experiment with canvas as an architectural material.

1932–1939 · Taliesin Fellowship Complex

Spring Green, Wisconsin

Wright at work in the Hillside drafting room.

The Hillside Home School Building of 1902 was adapted to become the Taliesin Fellowship Complex in 1932, when the Taliesin Fellowship was founded as a school for apprentice training in architecture. To the north of the original building was added the large drafting room, completed in 1939, with eight apprentice rooms along either side. Because of the intricate truss work of oak beams, Wright referred to this room as "the abstract forest." When this room was complete, all architectural work was moved over to Hillside from Taliesin, a quarter mile away, and the original Taliesin studio was then converted into Frank Lloyd Wright's personal office.

49

1934–1935 · Malcolm Willey House
Minneapolis, Minnesota

Exterior view

Two different designs were made for the Malcolm Willeys; the first one – a two-story residence with many features that would later evolve into the "Usonian House," proved too costly. The second one is a one-story plan called "The Garden Wall" because the building is placed along a brick wall at the far extremity of the property. This was done so as to take best advantage of the site. The floor is paved with brick, employing two different color tones set in alternating bands, as was done in the walls. The original furniture was a new direction in Wright's designs, and leads quite naturally into the plywood furniture he would later develop for the "Usonian" houses.

Opposite page:
Dining alcove in living room

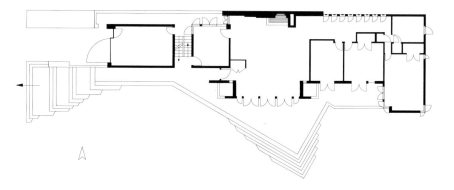

Plan

1935–1937 · Paul and Jean Hanna House

"Honeycomb House" ▸ Stanford, California

Opposite page:
Living room

In his continuing quest to find a more flexible plan form, one that would result likewise in more flexible interior space, Wright found the hexagon, and the hexagonal unit, more desirable than either the square or rectangle. In its first application at the house for Paul R. and Jean Hanna the hexagonal unit provides the basis for the plan. The house itself is not a hexagon, but has a free-flowing plan with wider angles (120 degrees) than the usual 90 degrees. Being a prototype, the project required a great number of architectural drawings to develop the scheme and then to produce a set of working drawings that could be easily understood by contractor and workmen.

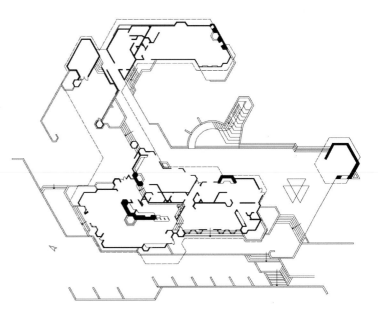

Plan

Perspective

1936–1939 · Johnson Building

S. C. Johnson & Son Company ▸ Racine, Wisconsin

When Wright's new administration building for the S. C. Johnson & Son Company opened its doors after three years of construction, it immediately created a sensation around the world. Life magazine featured it in its May 8, 1939 issue with remarks such as "Spectacular as the showiest Hollywood set, it represents simply the result of creative genius applied to the problem of designing the most efficient and comfortable, as well as beautiful, place in which Johnson Wax executives and clerks could do their work." The building was set in an industrial zone and Wright decided again to create an enclosed, sealed space and light it from above, as he had done in the Larkin Building. In the main workroom a forest of thin, white concrete columns rises to spread out at the top and forms the ceiling, the spaces in between the circles set with skylights made of glass tubes. At the corners, where the walls usually meet the ceiling, the walls stop short of the ceiling and glass tubes continue up, over, and connect to the skylights. The entrance is within the structure, penetrating the building on one side with a covered carport on the other. All the furniture, manufactured by Steelcase, was designed for the building. The warm, reddish brown hue of the bricks is used in the concrete floor slab as well; the white stone trim and white concrete columns make a subtle contrast.

Opposite page:
View at entrance

Great Workroom

Sun Trap living room in the detached residence for Wright's daughter
This is the site of the Wrights' residence before Taliesin West was built. Originally, this was a series of three "Sleeping Boxes," each made of wood and canvas with a bed, table, and wardrobe. These were grouped around a partially enclosed terrace with a large fireplace at one end. The original fireplace was later incorporated into Wright's design for his daughter's residence, seen here in the photograph.

Plan

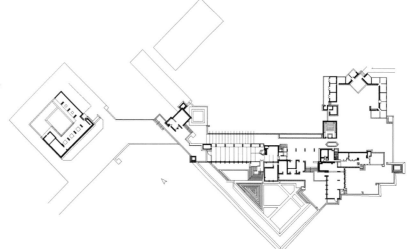

Drafting room interior

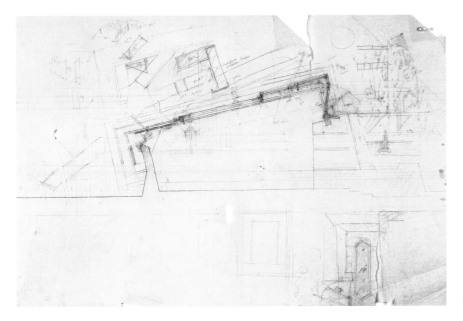

Garden room section

1938–1940 · John C. Pew House
Shorewood Hills, Wisconsin

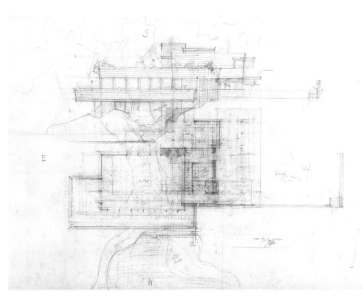

Drawing, preliminary sketch and elevation from the lakeside

The property John C. Pew chose for his Wisconsin house was narrow, with neighbors close by on either side. But the steep slope of the lot from the road above to the water's edge below and the profusion of trees and bushes made it possible for Wright to design a home that appears quite isolated and private. This was achieved by setting the house at an angle to the lake below, what the architect called "on the reflex." The building is really one large balcony composed of smaller ones, and the effect is not one of a house on a confined site, but of a house placed out and among the branches of the trees, looking down through the foliage onto the lake below.

Opposite page:
Lakeside view

1939–1940 · Rose Pauson House
Phoenix, Arizona

Opposite page:
View from the south

The perspective drawing for this work demonstrates the close, harmonious association of house and desert. It would seem, from this view, that the desert and dwelling were made at one and the same moment. Since the living room faced north, there was no need for an overhang, and the two-story glass gives a view onto a mountain range beyond. Rose Pauson and her sister Gertrude only lived in the house one season; when they returned to their native San Francisco, they rented the house, and it was destroyed by a fire. It was one of the most exquisite of Wright's residential works, its loss was indeed tragic.

Perspective sketch

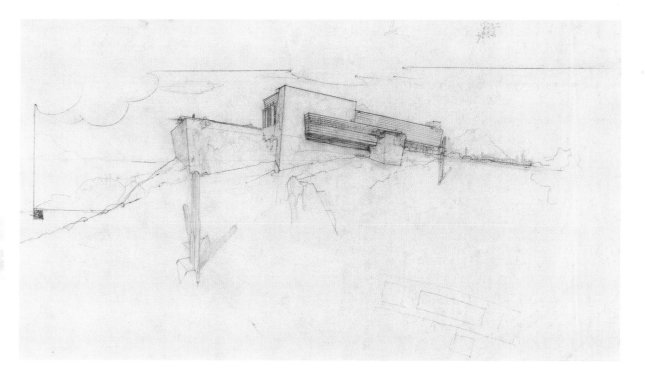

1943–1950 · Johnson Research Tower
S. C. Johnson & Son Company ▸ Racine, Wisconsin

When the S. C. Johnson & Son Company was contemplating the addition of a research laboratory to its plant in Racine, many of its officials considered the project one that any competent engineer could handle. But Herbert F. Johnson, who had commissioned Wright in 1936 for the office building, realized that any structure tangent to the famous administration building would have to respect the character of the former. "I had seen several meandering flat piles called laboratories," Wright wrote, "ducts running here, there and everywhere and a walkaround for everybody." The design he proposed consisted of fourteen levels, seven as square planes, with a circular mezzanine above each square level. The entire outside surface was sheathed in glass tubes, like the adjacent office structure, with plate glass clipped onto the inside surface for further insulation. "This seemed to me to be a natural solution and this sun-centered laboratory we now call the Heliolab came alive doing its own breathing and affording all kinds of delightful sun-lit, directly united, work space."

Cantilevered from the giant stack, the floor slabs spread out like tree branches, providing sufficient segregation of departments vertically. Elevator and stairway channels up the central stack, link all these departments to each other. Like the cellular pattern of the tree trunk, all utilities and the many laboratory intake and exhaust pipes run up and down in their own central utility groves. The single reinforced concrete foundation for this central core was termed "tap-root," and was based on an idea proposed by Frank Lloyd Wright for the St. Mark's Tower, New York, in 1929. Thus freed from peripheral supporting elements, the Tower rises gracefully from a garden and fountain pools that surround its base while a spacious court on three sides provides ample parking.

Street view

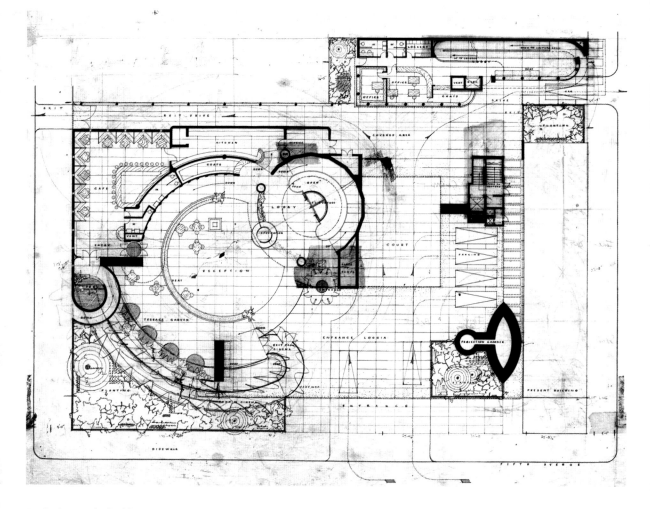

Plan for early proposal

April of 1959, the building was mainly complete, waiting for final details. Six months later, on October 21, the museum was opened to the world. While the building was in construction, a letter was sent to the director and trustees of the museum, signed by a long list of artists complaining that the sloped walls and ramped floor would be unsuitable for the exhibition of paintings. "Why do you think the walls of the Solomon R. Guggenheim Museum are gently sloping outward? They gently slope because the donor and his architect believed that pictures placed against the walls slightly tilted backward would be seen in better perspective and be better lighted than if set bolt upright. This is the chief characteristic of our building and was the hypothesis upon which the museum was fashioned. This idea is new but sound, one that can set a precedent of great value."

Opposite page:
Ground floor of rotunda

Opposite page:
Living room

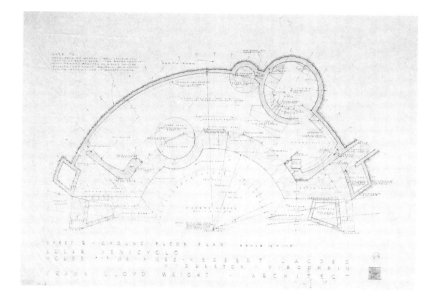

First floor plan

For a house in the northern climate, Wright devised a scheme that he named "Solar Hemicycle." The building for Herbert Jacobs is designed on a hemicycle plan, with earth piled up against the northern wall, in a berm, for insulation, with the southern wall composed of two-story glass windows and doors to bring in the sun's warmth in winter. The southern overhang is designed so that in summer shade is cast upon the glass, while in winter, the glass faces directly into the desired warmth of the sunshine, thus taking advantage of the elliptical solar path. The balcony, which contains the bedrooms, is hung from the ceiling rafters above by means of steel rods coming down through the partitions and locking into the floor beams. In this way, the space on the ground floor is altogether freed from any supports for the upper floor.

View towards entry
The house is entered through a tunnel that penetrates the berm on the north side of the house. Seen above on the right is the circular mass that contains the stairs and utilities on the ground floor, with stairs and bathroom on the mezzanine level. To the left and right of this mass are the high windows of the mezzanine bedrooms.

1947–1949 · Unitarian Church
Shorewood Hills, Wisconsin

The usual small or moderate-sized church in the United States at that time, 1947, was a slender Colonial box, a tall steeple on top of it, and frequently a Classical porch of some sort. Wright felt these forms to be highly inappropriate to the United States, or to the twentieth century. "In Unity Church here you see the Unitarianism of my fore-fathers found expression in a building by one of the offspring. The idea, 'unitarian,' was unity. Unitarians," he said, "believed in the unity of all things. Well, I tried to build a building here that expressed that over-all sense of unity. The plan you see is triangular. The roof is triangular and out of this – triangulation – (aspiration) you get this expression of reverence without recourse to the steeple." Wright frequently described the roof line of the church as like "the hands in an attitude of prayer."

Above:
Interior

Opposite page:
View from the east

1948–1950 · V. C. Morris Gift Shop
San Francisco, California

Since the Morris Shop on Maiden Lane, San Francisco, was built in 1949, and the Guggenheim Museum started construction in 1956, it is often and erroneously supposed that the design for the shop came before, and somewhat inspired, the design for the museum. It was in the museum, first designed in 1943, that Wright employed the interior ramp as a feature of the building. But in the Morris Shop the ramp is not so much a feature, although its presence dominates the sense of design inside, as it is a means of getting from ground floor up to second level. The entire shop is a remodeling of a previous space, but in place of the usual store front window, Wright has placed a blank brick curtain wall, with an arched opening of brick and glass.

The clients expressed some dismay about a gift shop without the customary display window on the street. Wright explained that in this design the merchandise was not to be pushed out onto the sidewalk, but rather the arched tunnel with the glass and a view into the shop would entice the shopper to peer in, see the items on the stone ledge displayed there under the arch, and then open the door. Wright humorously referred to this entrance as the "mouse trap." Once inside, a salesperson would greet the customer "Do come in, how may I serve you?"

Entrance

Opposite page:
Interior

1952–1956 · H.C. Price Company Tower
Bartlesville, Oklahoma

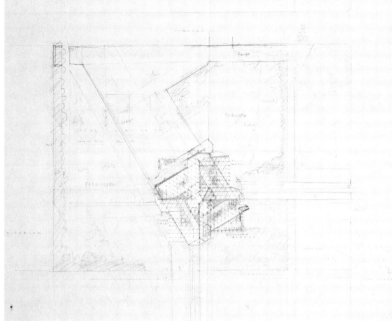

Above left:
Street view

Above right:
Sketch plan

Opposite page:
Perspective

The quadruple plan of the H. C. Price tower corresponds closely to the plan for the 1929 St. Mark's project, with one major difference: In St. Mark's there were duplex apartments in all four quadrants, while in the Price tower there are apartments in only one. Here, the other three quadrants of the tower serve as single-story office spaces. The H. C. Price Company occupied the top floors, with the sixteenth floor a buffet, kitchen, and outdoor terrace for dining and the 19th floor a private office for Harold Price.

There are eight duplex apartments that follow the St. Mark's plan: living room, kitchen, and lavatory on one level, stairs to the two bedrooms, and a bathroom on the mezzanine above. Both bedrooms have shutters that open onto the two-story living room. The master bedroom also opens onto a small outdoor balcony. In general, the office spaces are flexible, with movable partitions to serve the individual needs of each tenant. On the ground floor, the tower connects to a two-story structure, housing both a shop and the Public Service Company of Oklahoma. This connects to the northeast corner of the property.

The structure is all reinforced concrete with copper louvers and copper panels on the balconies. The windows on the three quadrants for offices have horizontal copper fins which shield the glass from direct sunlight. On the apartments, the two sides that rotate out from the square plan have vertical copper fins. The tower is positioned so that these vertical fins, or louvers, respond to the rotation of the earth and shade the glass in the summer months.

1954–1959·Synagogue

Beth Sholom Congregation ▸ Elkins Park, Pennsylvania

Interior

Opposite page:
Entrance

For the Beth Sholom Synagogue, Wright conceived a building that would be the very essence of light: a great translucent form rising out of concrete abutments. When the drawings were received by the rabbi, he immediately telegraphed Wright, "Sketches arrived safely. All deeply inspired by (their) beauty and majesty. Letter follows." In Cohen's long letter, written the next day, he further noted, "You have taken the supreme moment in Jewish history and experience – the revelation of God to Israel through Moses at Mt. Sinai and you have translated that moment with all it signifies into a design of beauty and reverence." The various sloping levels of the auditorium represent hands cupped loosely together. Wright called this "the congregation resting in the hands of God," while the projecting canopy over the entrance doors represents "the hands of the rabbi offering a benediction to his congregation as they enter the temple."

1956 ▸ Mile High Skyscraper
Project ▸ Chicago, Illinois

When the proposal to design a TV broadcasting tower one mile high was submitted to Wright, he believed it foolish to build such a tower without a building beneath it. Accordingly, on August 10, 1956 he created a conceptual sketch of an elevation that represents the rapier-like building growing slenderer as it rises, with a plan based on the form of a double-tripod. To explain the reason for the taper and the tripod, he said, "Does a church steeple sway in the wind? No, because the wind has no pressure on the top. That is why I made it the shape that it is. It is really a steeple and no wind pressure at the top, and as it comes down, even the shape of it defies wind pressure because you notice that it is a tetrahedron in form. It is really a tripod. Now the tripod is the surest form of resistance against outside pressure from the side because every pressure on every side is felt by the other sides and resisted by them altogether ... from whichever direction the wind comes, the two other sides stand braced against it."

On the same conceptual drawing he inscribed, "First 20 floors, 18' high, others, 10'. Total rentable area 6,000,000 square feet; deduct 2,000,000 sq. ft. for high rooms, studios, court rooms, audience halls, etc. Probable cost $60,000,000. Net 4,000,000 sq.ft. at $10 per sq.ft. Occupancy at 100 sq.ft. per person: 45,000 persons; transient occupancy in audience halls, etc. = 67,000 (approx.); total about 100,000 people. Parking 15,000 cars; 100 helicopters." Structural details were carefully considered as he developed the scheme: The foundation taproot plunges into bedrock like the handle of a sword, and the floors cantilever out from a central core, as seen in other towers of Wright's design. For further stability in this case, however, cables stretch down to the outer edges of the floors as in suspension bridges. The exterior wall surfaces are set well back beneath overhanging visors for protection against the sun and rain. The elevators are atomic powered vertical "trains," five cars tall, that run on ratchets like a cog railway. Since the building rises from five broad terraces at the base, the elevators correspond to the levels of the terraces. Although the basic building grows slenderer as it rises, the elevator shafts do not, and can be seen as they rise out of the building with corridors that connect to the various floor levels. The Mile High was never conceived of as a place to live, but rather as a place of work and social gathering. By clearing out the crowded city at the base and establishing a broad green park, even the traffic problem is alleviated.

Perspective

82

1959–1968 ▸ Norman Lykes House

Phoenix, Arizona

The Norman Lykes house was the last residential work designed by Frank Lloyd Wright. The site is a precipitous hillside overlooking Phoenix. The house was carefully situated so as not to disturb the terrain. It appears, in fact, to barely light upon the desert rocks. A large circular area for living room, dining room and work space affords the spectacular view south over the city and at the same time is engaged by a larger circle containing terrace and grass lawn. This spacious outdoor terrace is walled for privacy, the southern section pierced with openings to take advantage of the prospect. The bedroom wing arcs out from the living room, riding upon a crest of boulders.

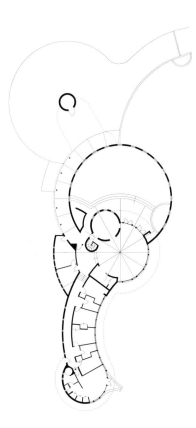

Plan

Street view

1957–1966 · Marin County Civic Center
San Rafael, California

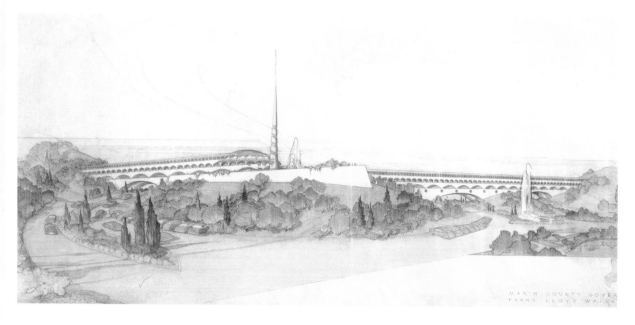

Perspective

The site of the Marin County Civic Center was a spacious, grassy park, with water lagoon, and four softly-molded hills. The building bridges across the hills with vistas of the park and water. While most government buildings in the United States are imposing, built on a vast scale, with a monumental aspect, the Marin County building is none of these. It puts mankind in a pleasing, human-scale environment exposed to the surrounding landscape. Running down the center of both buildings is an interior garden-court mall, lit by a skylight above. Offices are so planned that a view outside onto the hills is available in one direction, while a view into the skylighted interior mall is had in the other direction. Partitions for the various county offices are movable so as to accommodate the space requirement of each department for any specific year.

The Center is basically an elongated plan that changes direction at the central hill in order to bridge over to the next hills. The great arches at ground level support the structure, while the pendant arches above, hung from the edges of the floor slabs on the outdoor balconies, form sunshades for the windows which are set back five feet from the arches. Ease of access between departments is provided by these exterior balconies as well as the interior mall. The Hall of Justice meets the Administration Building in a circular junction, the third level of which provides a library. On a second level there is a cafeteria which opens onto a triangular prow in which there is a paved terrace for outdoor dining, a garden, and a pool. An important feature of the building is the gold-anodized aluminum balcony railing on the third level which casts ever moving shadow patterns on the walls. Wright frequently called patterns of this nature, caused by architectural features, "eye music."

Opposite page:
Side view of pendant arches

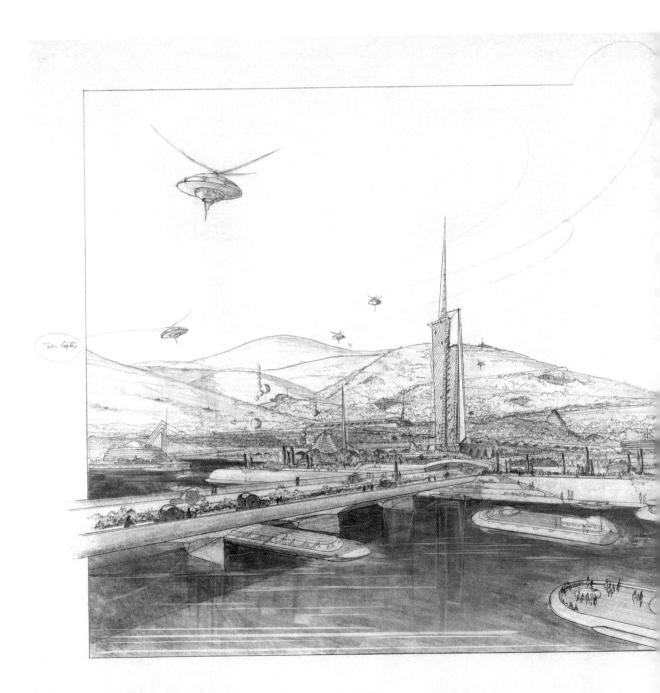

1958 · The Living City
Project

In 1932, Wright published *The Disappearing City*, a book in which he expounded the need for decentralization, the need to move out of the polluted and crowded cities and into the landscape of the countryside. Cognizant of the enormous amount of available land nationwide, he proposed a utopian solution he called "Broadacre City." Two years later, he prepared a twelve-foot square model of Broadacre City that toured the States. In 1945, he revised *The Disappearing City* and retitled it *When Democracy Builds*, illustrated by photographs of the model and other ancillary models related to it. His deeply felt conviction about the unhealthy environment of cities never left him. As early as 1931 he wrote, "Is the city a natural triumph of the herd instinct over humanity, and therefore a temporal necessity as a hangover from the infancy of the race, to be outgrown as humanity grows? ... I believe the city, as we know it today, is to die. We are witnessing the acceleration that precedes dissolution."

In 1958, he returned to the idea of Broadacre City and again revised his thesis in the book *The Living City*. For this publication, Wright had his apprentices produce several perspective drawings of a hypothetical "city" set in a landscape of rolling hills, expansive prairies, lakes, and rivers. In *The Living City*, "Atomic Barges" and "Taxi Copters" provide futuristic transport, while, in and amongst the natural landscape, buildings of his own design, both built and unbuilt appear: Marin County Civic Center, Beth Sholom Synagogue, Price Tower, the Rogers Lacy Hotel, the Gordon Strong Automobile Objective and Planetarium, the Kaufmann Pittsburgh Self-Service Garage, as well as the Pittsburgh Point Park Civic Center and Huntington Hartford Sports Club and Play Resort. Here he has illustrated his solution for a city that is healthy, humane, and beautiful.

Sketch

House for Warren Hickox, Kankakee, IL
House Remodeling for E. R. Hills, Oak Park, IL
House Remodeling for Warren McArthur, Chicago, IL
Summer Cottage for E. H. Pitkin, Sapper Island, Desbarats, Ontario, Canada
Cottage for Henry Wallis, Lake Delavan, WI

1901 ▸ Wright reads his lecture *The Art and Craft of the Machine* at Hull House in Chicago.
House for E. Arthur Davenport, River Forest, IL
House for William G. Fricke, Oak Park, IL
House Remodeling for Dr. A. W. Hebert, Evanston, IL
House for F. B. Henderson, Elmhurst, IL
Boathouse for Fred B. Jones, Lake Delavan, WI
House for Fred B. Jones, Lake Delavan, WI
River Forest Golf Club Additions, River Forest, IL
House for Frank Thomas, Oak Park, IL
Exhibition Pavilion for Universal Portland Cement Company, Buffalo, NY
Poultry House, Stables and Gates for Edward C. Waller, River Forest, IL
Gatehouse for Henry Wallis, Lake Delavan, WI
Stables for T. E. Wilder, Elmhurst, IL
Barn, Stables and Gatehouse for Fred B. Jones, Lake Delavan, WI

1902
Delavan Yacht Club, Lake Delavan, WI
Double Cottage for George Gerts, Whitehall, MI
Cottage for Walter Gerts, Whitehall, MI
House for Arthur Heurtley, Oak Park, IL
House Remodeling for Arthur Heurtley, Les Cheneaux Club, Marquette Island, MI
Hillside Home School Rebuilding, Spring Green, WI
House for Francis W. Little, Peoria, IL
House for Charles R. Ross, Lake Delavan, WI
House for George W. Spencer, Lake Delavan, WI
House for Ward W. Willits, Highland Park, IL
House for Susan Lawrence Dana, Springfield, IL

1903 ▸ Son Robert Llewellyn Wright born.
Abraham Lincoln Center for Jenkin Lloyd Jones, Chicago, IL
House for George Barton, Buffalo, NY
House for Edwin H. Cheney, Oak Park, IL
House for W. H. Freeman, Hinsdale, IL
Larkin Company Administration Building, Buffalo, NY
Scoville Park Fountain, Oak Park, IL
House for J. J. Walser, Chicago, IL
House for William E. Martin, Oak Park, IL
House for Robert M. Lamp, Madison, WI
House for Darwin D. Martin, Buffalo, NY
House for William R. Heath, Buffalo, NY

1904 ▸ Wright attends the Louisiana Purchase Exposition in Saint Louis.

1905 ▸ Wright and his wife, Catherine, make their first trip to Japan, accompanied by Wright's clients Mr. and Mrs. Ward Willits. Wright begins collecting and dealing in Japanese prints.
House for Mary M. W. Adams, Highland Park, IL
House for Charles E. Brown, Evanston, IL
Real Estate Office for E. A. Cummings, River Forest, IL
E-Z Polish Factory for William E. and Darwin D. Martin, Chicago, IL
Three Summer Cottages for Mrs. Thomas Gale, Whitehall, MI
House for W. A. Glasner, Glencoe, IL
House for Thomas P. Hardy, Racine, WI
House for A. P. Johnson, Lake Delavan, WI
Lawrence Memorial Library, Springfield, IL
Gardener's Cottage for D. D. Martin, Buffalo, NY
River Forest Tennis Club, River Forest, IL
Rookery Building, Interior Remodeling, Chicago, IL
Bank for Frank L. Smith, Dwight, IL
Unity Temple, Oak Park, IL
House for Harvey Sutton, McCook, NE

1906 ▸ Wright exhibits his collection of Hiroshige prints at the Art Institute of Chicago.
House Remodelling for P. A. Beachy, Oak Park, IL
House for K. C. DeRhodes, South Bend, IN
House for A. W. Gridley, Batavia, IL
House for P. D. Hoyt, Geneva, IL
House for George M. Millard, Highland Park, IL
House for Frederick Nicholas, Flossmoor, IL
Pettit Mortuary Chapel, Belvidere, IL
Tennis Club Rebuilding, River Forest, IL

1907
House for Avery Coonley, Riverside, IL
House Remodeling for Col. George Fabyan, Geneva, IL
Fox River Country Club Remodeling, Geneva, IL
House for Stephen M. M. Hunt, La Grange, IL
Larkin Company Exhibition Pavilion, Jamestown, VA
Emma Martin House House, Oak Park, IL
Pebbles and Balch Remodelled Shop, Oak Park, IL
"Tanyderi," House for Andrew Porter, Hillside, Spring Green, WI
House for F. F. Tomek, Riverside, IL
House for Barton J. Westcott, Springfield, OH
Garage Additions for George Blossom, Chicago, IL
House for E. E. Boynton, Rochester, NY
Gardener's Cottage and Stables for Avery Coonley, Riverside, IL

1908 ▸ German philosopher Kuno Francke meets with Wright in Oak Park; the Wasmuth portfolio would be the result of this meeting.
Browne's Bookstore, Chicago, IL

House for Walter V. Davidson, Buffalo, NY
House for Robert W. Evans, Chicago, IL
House for Eugene A. Gilmore, Madison, WI
House for L. K. Horner, Chicago, IL
House for Meyer May, Grand Rapids, MI
House for Isabel Roberts, River Forest, IL
House for Dr. G. C. Stockman, Mason City, IA
House for Frederick C. Robie, Chicago, IL

1909 ▸ Wright leaves his practice and family for Europe, accompanied by Mamah Borthwick Cheney.
House for Frank J. Baker, Wilmette, IL
Bitter Root Inn, near Darby, MT
City National Bank and Hotel, Mason City, IA
Robert Clark House, Peoria, IL
House Remodeling for Dr. W. H. Copeland, scheme 2, Oak Park, IL
House for Mrs. Thomas Gale, Oak Park, IL
House for J. Kibben Ingalls, River Forest, IL
House for Oscar M. Steffens, Chicago, IL
House for George Stewart, Montecito, CA
Stohr Arcade and Shops, Chicago, IL
Thurber's Art Gallery, Fine Arts Building, Chicago, IL
Bathing Pavilion for Edward C. Waller, Charlevoix, MI
House for Hiram Baldwin, Kenilworth, IL
Como Orchards Summer Colony, Darby, MT
House for Ingwald Moe, Evanston, IL

1910 ▸ Wright travels to Berlin and then to Fiesole. In Fiesole, Wright, son Lloyd, and draftsman Taylor Woolley prepare the illustrations for *Ausgeführte Bauten und Entwürfe*, published that year in Berlin by Ernst Wasmuth.
Blythe-Markeley Law Office, City National Bank Building, Mason City, IA
House for E. P. Irving, Decatur, IL
Universal Portland Cement Company Exhibition Pavilion, Madison Square Garden, New York, NY
House for Reverend J. R. Ziegler, Frankfort, KY

1911 ▸ Wright begins building a new home and studio near Spring Green, WI. The complex is called Taliesin.
House for Herbert Angster, Lake Bluff, IL
Pavilion, Banff National Park, Alberta, Canada
Lake Geneva Inn, Lake Geneva, WI
Taliesin I, Spring Green, WI
Taliesin Hydro House, Spring Green, WI
Oak Park Home and Studio Remodeling for Frank Lloyd Wright, Oak Park, IL
Remodeling of Stables for Avery Coonley, Riverside, IL
House for O. B. Balch, Oak Park, IL
Taliesin Dam, Spring Green, WI

1912 ▸ Wright publishes *The Japanese Print:*

An Interpretation.
House for William B. Greene, Aurora, IL
"Northome," House for Francis W. Little, Wayzata, MN
Park Ridge Country Club Remodeling, Park Ridge, IL
Stables and Garage for Sherman Booth, Glenoe, IL
Playhouse for Avery Coonley, Riverside, IL

1913 ► Wright visits Japan to secure the commission for the Imperial Hotel and to acquire Japanese prints for American clients.
House for Harry S. Adams, Oak Park, IL
Midway Gardens, Chicago, IL

1914 ► Julian Carlston kills Mamah Cheney and six others, then sets fire to Taliesin. Wright meets Miriam Noel.

1915
House for Emil Bach, Chicago, IL
House for Sherman Booth, Glencoe, IL
House for E. D. Brigham, Glencoe, IL
A. D. German Warehouse, Richland Center, WI
Ravine Bluffs Bridge, Glencoe, IL
Ravine Bluffs Housing, Glencoe, IL
American Homes for the Richards Company (ARCS), Milwaukee, WI
Duplex Apartments for Arthur Munkwitz (ARCS), Milwaukee, WI
Duplex Apartments for Arthur L. Richards (ARCS), Milwaukee, WI
Small House for the Richards Company (ARCS), Milwaukee, WI

1916 ► Wright signs contract for the design for the new Imperial Hotel; opens an office in Tokyo.
House for Joseph Bagley, Grand Beach, MI
House for Frederick C. Bogk, Milwaukee, WI
House for W. S. Carr, Grand Beach, MI
House for Ernest Vosburgh, Grand Beach, MI
Imperial Hotel, Tokyo, Japan

1917
"Hollyhock House" for Aline Barnsdall, Olive Hill, Los Angeles, CA
House for Aisaku Hayashi, Tokyo, Japan
House for Stephen M. B. Hunt, Oshkosh, WI
House for Henry J. Allen, Wichita, KS
House for Arinobu Fukuhara, Hakone, Japan

1918 ► Wright goes to Peiping, China to commission rugs for Imperial Hotel. On the same trip he visits Seoul, Korea. He visits the monuments and art treasures as a guest of the writer Ku Hung Ming.

1920

"Residence A" and "Residence B" for Aline Barnsdall, Olive Hill, Los Angeles, CA
Imperial Hotel Annex, Tokyo, Japan

1921
Jiyu Gakuen School, Tokyo, Japan

1922 ► Wright opens an office in Los Angeles. Wright and Catherine are divorced.
House for Tazaemon Yamamura, Ashiya, Japan

1923 ► Kanto earthquake demolishes much of Tokyo. The Imperial Hotel survives. Wright publishes *Experimenting with Human Lives* concerning the earthquake and the Imperial Hotel. He marries Miriam Noel.
House for Charles Ennis, Los Angeles, CA
House for Samuel Freeman, Los Angeles, CA
"La Miniatura," House for Alice Millard, Pasadena, CA
House Rebuilding for Nathan G. Moore, Oak Park, IL
House for John Storer, Los Angeles, CA
"Little Dipper" Kindergarten for Aline Barnsdall, Olive Hill, Los Angeles, CA

1924 ► Wright meets Olgivanna Lazovich Hinzenburg.

1925 ► Second major fire occurs at Taliesin. Daughter Iovanna born to Frank Lloyd Wright and Olgivanna Hinzenburg.
Taliesin III, Spring Green, WI

1926 ► The Bank of Wisconsin takes title to Taliesin, due to Wright's indebtedness. Wright and Hinzenburg are arrested near Minneapolis for allegedly violating the Mann Act.
"Greycliff," House for Isabelle Martin (Mrs. D. D. Martin), Derby, NY

1927 ► Wright begins a series of articles under the heading *In the Cause of Architecture*, subsequently published in *The Architectural Record*. Wright divorces Miriam Noel Wright.

1928 ► Wright marries Olgivanna Hinzenburg.

1929 ► Work continues on projects for Chandler, but following stock-market crash on October, these projects come to a halt.
Camp Cabins for the Chandler Land Improvement Co., Chandler, AZ
House for Richard Lloyd Jones, Tulsa, OK
"Ocatillo," Frank Lloyd Wright Desert Compound and Studio, near Chandler, AZ

1930 ► Wright delivers the Kahn Lectures at

Princeton University and publishes them under the title *Modern Architecture*. Large Exhibition of his work tours Princeton, New York, Chicago, Madison and Milwaukee.

1931 ► Exhibition tours Eugene, OR and then goes overseas to Amsterdam, Berlin, Stuttgart, Antwerp, and Brussels.

1932 ► The Wrights found the Taliesin Fellowship and convert the Hillside Home School buildings into the Taliesin Fellowship Complex. Wright publishes *An Autobiography* and *The Disappearing City*. Exhibition of Wright's work included in *The International Style* at The Museum of Modern Art, New York City.
Taliesin Fellowship Complex, Spring Green, WI

1933
Hillside Playhouse, Taliesin, Spring Green, WI

1934 ► Wright and apprentices begin construction of a scale model of Broadacre City. The first issue of *Taliesin*, a magazine founded by Wright is published by the Taliesin Press.
House for Malcolm Willey, Minneapolis, MN

1935 ► The completed model of Broadacre City is exhibited at the Industrial Arts Exposition at the Rockefeller Center, New York City.
"Fallingwater," House for Edgar J. Kaufmann, Mill Run, PA
"Honeycomb House" for Paul R. and Jean Hanna, Stanford, CA
Office for Edgar J. Kaufmann, Kaufmann's Department Store, Pittsburgh, PA

1936
House for Herbert Jacobs, Madison, WI
S. C. Johnson & Son Company Administration Building, Racine, WI
"Deertrack," House for Mrs. Abby Beecher Roberts, Marquette, MI

1937 ► Wright and author Baker Brownell write and publish *Architecture and Modern Life*.
"Wingspread," House for Herbert F. Johnson, Wind Point, WI
House for Ben Rebhuhn, Great Neck Estates, NY
Taliesin West, Scottsdale, AZ

1938 ► Wright designs the January issue of Architectural Forum, which is dedicated to his work and appears on the cover of *Time* magazine.
Florida Southern College Master Plan for Dr. Ludd M. Spivey, Lakeland, FL
Anne Pfeiffer Chapel, Florida Southern College,

Anne Pfeiffer Chapel, Florida Southern College, Lakeland, FL
Guest House for Edgar J. Kaufmann, Mill Run, PA
House for Charles L. Manson, Wausau, WI
Midway Barns and Farm Buildings, Taliesin, Spring Green, WI
House for John C. Pew, Shorewood Hills, WI
Sun Top Homes for Otto Mallery and the Todd Company, Ardmore, PA

1939 ▸ Wright is invited to London to deliver a series of lectures at The Sulgrave Manor Board. They are published as *An Organic Architecture.*
House for Andrew F. H. Armstrong, Ogden Dunes, IN
House for Sidney Bazett, Hillsborough, CA
House for Joseph Euchtman, Baltimore, MD
House for Lloyd Lewis, Libertyville, IL
House for Rose Pauson, Phoenix, AZ
House for Loren Pope, Falls Church, VA
House for Stanley Rosenbaum, Florence, AL
House for Bernard Schwartz, Two Rivers, WI
House for Clarence Sondern, Kansas City, MO
"Auldbrass," House and Adjuncts for Leigh Stevens, Yemassee, SC
House for George Sturges, Brentwood Heights, CA
House for Kathrine Winckler and Alma Goetsch, Okemos, MI

1940 ▸ *The Work of Frank Lloyd Wright*, a major retrospective exhibition is held at The Museum of Modern Art, New York City, NY.
House for Gregor Affleck, Bloomfield Hills, MI
House for Theodore Baird, Amherst, MA
House for James Christie, Bernardsville, NJ
Community Church, Kansas City, MO
Seminar Buildings, Florida Southern College, Lakeland, FL
Gatehouse for Arch Oboler, Malibu, CA
"Eleanor's Retreat" for Arch Obeler, Malibu, CA

1941 ▸ Wright and Frederick Gutheim publish *On Architecture.*
Roux Library, Florida Southern College, Lakeland, FL
House for Stuart Richardson, Glen Ridge, NJ
"Snowflake," House for C. D. Wall, Plymouth, MI

1942
Industrial Arts Building, Florida Southern College, Lakeland, FL

1943
Solomon R. Guggenheim Museum, New York, NY
Poultry Shed for Lloyd Lewis, Libertyville, IL
S. C. Johnson & Son Company Research Tower, Racine, WI

1944
Hillside Theatre Foyer, Spring Green, WI
"Solar Hemicycle," House for Herbert Jacobs # 2, Middleton, WI
Addition to Midway Barns, Farm Building at Taliesin, Spring Green, WI

1945 ▸ Wright publishes *When Democracy Builds.*
Administration Building, Florida Southern College, Lakeland, FL
Lodge for Arnold Friedman, Pecos, NM
Solomon R. Guggenheim Museum, revised scheme, New York, NY
House for Lowell Walter, Cedar Rock, Quasqueton, IA

1946
House for Amy Alpaugh, Northport, MI
Esplanades, Florida Southern College, Lakeland, FL
House for Douglas Grant, Cedar Rapids, IA
House for Chauncey Griggs, Tacoma, WA
Additions to House for Paul R. and Jean Hanna, Stanford, CA
House for Dr. Alvin Miller, Charles City, IA
House for Herman T. Mossberg, South Bend, IN
House for Melvyn Maxwell Smith, Bloomfield Hills, MI
Additions to House for Stanley Rosenbaum, Florence, AL

1947
House for Carroll Alsop, Oskaloosa, IA
House for Dr. A. H. Bulbulian, Rochester, MN
Dairy and Machine Shed, Midway Barns, Taliesin, Spring Green, WI
Galesburg Country Homes, Master Plan, Galesburg, MI
Additions to Guest House for Edgar J. Kaufmann, Mill Run, PA
Parkwyn Village Housing, Master Plan, Kalamazoo, MI
Unitarian Church, Shorewood Hills, WI
Usonia II Housing, Master Plan, Pleasantville, NY
House for Jack Lamberson, Oskaloosa, IA
House for Charles T. Weltzheimer, Oberlin, OH
Sun Trap for Iovanna Lloyd Wright, Taliesin West, Scottsdale, AZ

1948
House for Erling Brauner, Okemos, MI
House for Maynard Buehler, Orinda, CA
House for Samuel Eppstein, Galesburg, MI
House for Sol Friedman, Pleasantville, NY
House for Robert Levin, Kalamazoo, MI
House for Curtis Meyer, Galesburg, MI
Gift Shop for V. C. Morris, San Francisco, CA
House for Eric Pratt, Galesburg, MI

Boathouse and River Pavilion for Lowell Walter, Quasqueton, IA
House for David Weisblatt, Galesburg, MI
House for Albert Adelman, Fox Point, WI
House for Mrs. Clinton Walker, Carmel, CA

1949
House for Howard Anthony, Benton Harbor, MI
House for Eric Brown, Kalamazoo, MI
Cabaret Theater, Taliesin West, Scottsdale, AZ
House for James Edwards, Okemos, MI
House for J. Willis Hughes, Jackson, MS
House for Kenneth Laurent, Rockford, IL
House for Ward McCartney, Kalamazoo, MI
House for Henry J. Neils, Minneapolis, MN
House for Edward Serlin, Pleasantville, NY
Additions to Sondern House for Arnold Adler, Kansas City, MO

1950
House for Robert Berger, San Anselmo, CA
House for Raymond Carlson, Phoenix, AZ
House for John O. Carr, Glenview, IL
House for Dr. Richard Davis, Marion, IN
House for S. P. Elam, Austin, MN
House for John A. Gillin, Dallas, TX
House for Dr. Ina Harper, St. Joseph, MI
House for John Haynes, Fort Wayne, IN
House for Thomas E. Keys, Rochester, MN
House for Arthur Mathews, Atherton, CA
House for Robert Muirhead, Plato Center, IL
House for William Palmer, Ann Arbor, MI
House for Wilbur Pearce, Bradbury, CA
House for Don Schaberg, Okemos, MI
House for Seymour Shavin, Chattanooga, TN
House for Richard Smith, Jefferson, WI
House for Karl A. Staley, North Madison, OH
House for J. A. Sweeton, Cherry Hill, NJ
House for Robert Winn, Kalamazoo, MI
House for David Wright, "How to live in the Southwest", Phoenix, AZ
House for Isadore Zimmerman, Manchester, NH

1951 ▸ Wright and his apprentices design and construct an exhibition of Wright's work entitled "Sixty Years of Living Architecture." This show opens in Philadelphia and then travels to the Palazzo Strozzi in Florence. Wright opens West Coast office in San Francisco with Aaron Green, Associate.
House for Benjamin Adelman, Phoenix, AZ
House for Gabrielle Austin, Greenville, SC
Summer Cottage for A. K. Chahroudi, Lake Mahopac, NY
House for W. L. Fuller, Pass Christian, MS
House for Charles F. Glore, Lake Forest, IL
S. C. Johnson & Son Co. Additions, Racine, WI

House for Patrick Kinney, Lancaster, WI
House for Russell Kraus, Kirkwood, MO
House for Roland Reisley, Pleasantville, NY
House for Dr. Nathan Rubin, Canton, OH

1952 ▶ A fire partly destroys Wright's Hillside Home School buildings in Spring Green. Exhibition "Sixty Years of Living Architecture" travels to Switzerland, France, Germany and Holland.
Anderton Court Shops, Beverly Hills, CA
House for Quintin Blair, Cody, WY
House for Ray Brandes, Issaquah, WA
Hillside Theater, Spring Green, WI
House for George Lewis, Tallahassee, FL
House for R. W. Lindholm, Cloquet, MN
House for Louis Penfield, Willoughby Hills, OH
House for Arthur Pieper, Paradise Valley, AZ
Harold C. Price Company Tower, Bartlesville, OK
House for Frank Sander, Stamford, CT
Studio-Residence for Archie Teater, Bliss, ID
Caretaker's House for Arnold Friedman, Pecos, NM
Office for Aaron G. Green, San Francicso, CA

1953 ▶ Wright publishes The Future of Architecture. Exhibition "Sixty Years of Living Architecture" travels to Mexico City and New York.
Cottage for Jorgine Boomer, Phoenix, AZ
House for Andrew B. Cooke, Virginia Beach, VA
House for John Dobkins, Canton, OH
Science and Cosmography Building, Florida Southern College, Lakeland, FL
House for Lewis Goddard, Plymouth, MI
House for Harold Price, Jr., Bartlesville, OK
Riverview Terrace Restaurant, Spring Green, WI
Pavilion and Usonian House for "Sixty Years of Living Architecture" New York, NY
House for William Thaxton, Houston, TX
House for Luis Marden, McLean, VA

1954 ▶ Wright publishes The Natural House.
House for E. Clarke Arnold, Columbus, WI
House for Bachman and Wilson, Millstone, NJ
Beth Sholom Synagogue, Elkins Park, PA
House for Cedric Boulter, Cincinnati, OH
House for John E. Christian, West Lafayette, IN
House for Ellis Feiman, Canton, OH
Danforth Chapel, Florida Southern College, Lakeland, FL
House for Louis B. Frederick, Barrington Hill, IL
House for Dr. Maurice Greenberg, Dousman, WI
House for I. N. Hagan, Chalkhill, PA
Jaguar Showroom for Max Hoffman, New York, NY
House for Willard Keland, Racine, WI
"Grandma House" for Harold Price, Paradise Valley, AZ
House for Gerald Tonkens, Cincinnati, OH

House for W. B. Tracy, Normandy Park, WA
Guest House for David Wright, Phoenix, AZ
Hotel Plaza Apartment Remodelling for Frank Lloyd Wright, New York, NY
Pavillon for the exhibition "Sixty Years of Living Architecture", Hollyhock House, Los Angeles, CA

1955 ▶ Wright publishes An American Architecture, edited by Edgar Kaufmann, jr.
Kalita Humphreys Theater, Dallas Theater Center, for Paul Baker, Dallas, TX
House for Randall Fawcett, Los Banos, CA
House for Max Hoffman, Rye, NY
House for Dr. Toufic Kalil, Manchester, NH
Kundert Medical Clinic, San Luis Obispo, CA
House for Don Lovness, Stillwater, MN
House for T. A. Pappas, St. Louis, MO
House for John Rayward, New Canaan, CT
Remodelling of the Isabel Roberts House for Warren Scott, River Forest, IL
House for Robert Sunday, Marshalltown, IA
House for Dr. Dorothy Turkel, Detroit, MI
Heritage Henredon Fine Furniture, "Four Square," Morganton, NC
Fabrics and Wall Coverings for F. Schumacher & Son, "Taliesin Line," New York, NY
Color Palette for Martin-Senour Paint Company, "Taliesin Palette," Chicago, IL

1956 ▶ Mayor Richard Daley of Chicago declares October 17 "Frank Lloyd Wright Day." Wright publishes The Story of the Tower.
Annunciation Greek Orthodox Church, Wauwatosa, WI
House for William Boswell, Cincinnati, OH
House for Frank Bott, Kansas City, MO
House for Allen Friedman, Bannockburn, IL
Solomon R. Guggenheim Museum, final revised scheme, New York, NY
Additions to House for Paul R. and Jean Hanna, Stanford, CA
Lindholm Service Station, Cloquet, MN
Clinic for Dr. Kenneth Meyers, Dayton, OH
Music Pavilion, Taliesin West, Scottsdale, AZ
Remodeling of the Frank Lloyd Wright Home and Studio for Clyde Nooker, Oak Park, IL
House for Dudley Spencer, Brandywine Head, DE
House for Dr. Paul Trier, Des Moines, IA
Wyoming Valley School, Wyoming Valley, near Spring Green, WI
House for Robert Llewellyn Wright, Bethesda, MD
Pre-Fabricated House #1 for Marshall Erdmann and Associetes, Inc., Madison, WI
House for C. E. Gordon, Aurora, OR

1957 ▶ Wright is invited to Baghdad, Iraq, to design an opera house, cultural center, mu-

seum, university, and postal-telegraph building. Wright publishes A Testament.
Clinic for Herman Fasbender, Hastings, MN
House for Sterling Kinney, Amarillo, TX
Marin County Civic Center, San Rafael, CA
Playhouse for Victoria and Jennifer Rayward, New Canaan, CT
House for Carl Schultz, St. Joseph, MI
House for Dr. Robert Walton, Modesto, CA
House for Duey Wright, Wausau, WI
Pre-Fabricated House #2 for Marshall Erdmann and Associates, Inc., Madison, WI
Marin County Post Office, Marin County Civic Center, San Rafael, CA

1958 ▶ Wright publishes The Living City.
House for Dr. George Ablin, Bakersfield, CA
Juvenile Cultural Study Center, Building A, University of Wichita, Wichita, KS
Lockridge Medical Clinic, Whitefish, MT
House for Paul Olfelt, St. Louis Park, MN
Cottage for Seth C. Petersen, Lake Delton, WI
Pilgrim Congregational Church, Redding, CA
Additions to House for John Rayward, New Canaan, CT
House for Don Stromquist, Bountiful, UT

1959 ▶ Wright dies April 9.
Grady Gammage Memorial Auditorium, Arizona State University, Tempe, AZ
House for Norman Lykes, Phoenix, AZ

USA

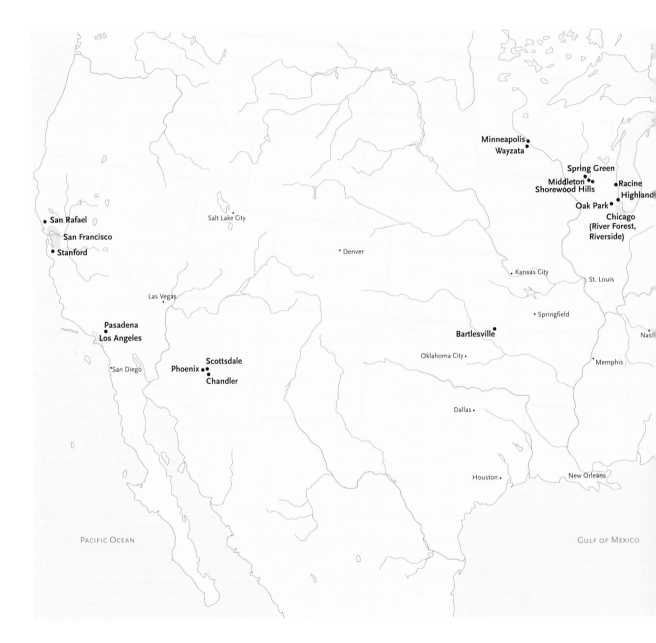

Minneapolis
Wayzata

Spring Green
Middleton
Shorewood Hills
Oak Park
Racine
Highland
Chicago
(River Forest,
Riverside)

San Rafael
San Francisco
Stanford

Salt Lake City

Denver

Kansas City

St. Louis

Springfield

Nas

Las Vegas

Pasadena
Los Angeles

San Diego

Phoenix
Scottsdale
Chandler

Bartlesville

Oklahoma City

Memphis

Dallas

Houston

New Orleans

PACIFIC OCEAN

GULF OF MEXICO

Bartlesville, Oklahoma
H.C. Price Company Tower

Buffalo, New York
Larkin Building, Company Administration
Building

near Chandler, Arizona
"Ocatillo", Frank Lloyd Wright Desert Compound

Chicago, Illinois
Frederick C. Robie House
Mile High Skyscraper

Elkins Park, Pennsylvania
Synagogue, Beth Sholom Congregation

Highland Park, Illinois
Ward W. Willits House

Los Angeles, California
Charles Ennis House
"Hollyhock House", Aline Barnsdall House

Middleton, Wisconsin
"Solar Hemicycle", Herbert Jacobs House

Mill Run, Pennsylvania
"Fallingwater", Edgar J. Kaufmann House

Minneapolis, Minnesota
Malcolm Willey House

New York, New York
Guggenheim Museum

Oak Park, Illinois
Mrs. Thomas Gale House
Unity Temple
William Fricke House

Pasadena, California
"La Miniatura", Alice Millard House

Phoenix, Arizona
Norman Lykes House
Rose Pauson House

Racine, Wisconsin
Johnson Building, S. C. Johnson & Son Company
Johnson Research Tower, S. C. Johnson & Son
Company

River Forest, Illinois
William H. Winslow House

Riverside, Illinois
Avery Coonley House
Avery Coonley Playhouse

San Francisco, California
V. C. Morris Gift Shop

San Rafael, California
Marin County Civic Centre

Scottsdale, Arizona
Taliesin West, Frank Lloyd Wright Home and
Studio

Shorewood Hills, Wisconsin
John C. Pew House
Unitarian Church

Spring Green, Wisconsin
Taliesin, Frank Lloyd Wright House, Studio and
Farm
Taliesin Fellowship Complex

Stanford, California
"Honeycomb House", Jean and Paul Hanna
House

Wayzata, Minnesota
"Northome", Francis W. Little House

Bibliography

Credits

▶ Alofsin, Anthony: Frank Lloyd Wright, The Lost Years, 1910–1922. University of Chicago Press, Chicago & London, 1993
▶ Brooks, H. Allen: The Prairie School, Frank Lloyd Wright And His Midwest Contemporaries. George Braziller, New York, 1984
▶ Cleary, Richard: Merchant Prince and Master Builder, Edgar Kaufmann & Frank Lloyd Wright. Carnegie Museum of Art, Pittsburgh, 1999
▶ De Long, David: Frank Lloyd Wright, Designs for an American Landscape. Harry N. Abrams, New York, 1995
▶ De Long, David (ed.): Frank Lloyd Wright and the Living City. Vitra Design Museum/Skira editore, Weil am Rhein, 1998
▶ Futagawa, Yukio (ed.): Frank Lloyd Wright Monograph. 12 Volumes. A.D.A. Edita, Tokyo, 1986
▶ Gebhard, David: California Romanza, The California Architecture of Frank Lloyd Wright. Chronicle Press, San Francisco, 1988
▶ Guerrero, Pedro E.: Picturing Wright, An Album from Frank Lloyd Wright's Photographer. Pomegranate Artbooks, San Francisco, 1994
▶ Hanks, David A.: Decorative Designs of Frank Lloyd Wright. Dover Books, New York, 1999
▶ Hildebrand, Grant: The Wright Space, Pattern & Meaning in Frank Lloyd Wright's Houses. University of Washington Press, Seattle, 1991
▶ Hitchcock, Henry Russell: Frank Lloyd Wright, In the Nature of Materials 1887–1941. Da Capo Press, New York, 1988
▶ Kaufmann, Edgar jr. (ed.): An American Architecture. Barnes & Noble, New York, 1998
▶ Levine, Neil: The Architecture of Frank Lloyd Wright. Princeton University Press, Princeton, 1996
▶ Manson, Grant Carpenter: Frank Lloyd Wright to 1910, The First Golden Age. John Wiley & Sons, New York, 1979
▶ McCarter, Robert: Frank Lloyd Wright. Phaidon Press Ltd., London, 1997
▶ Pfeiffer, Bruce Brooks: Frank Lloyd Wright, The Masterworks. Rizzoli, New York, 1993
▶ Pfeiffer, Bruce Brooks: Frank Lloyd Wright, Master Builder. Universe Publishing Co., New York, 1997
▶ Pfeiffer, Bruce Brooks: Treasures Of Taliesin, 77 Unbuilt Designs. Pomegranate, San Francisco, 1999

▶ Pfeiffer, Bruce Brooks (ed.): Frank Lloyd Wright, In the Realm of Ideas. Southern Illinois University Press, Carbondale & Edwardsville, 1988
▶ Pfeiffer, Bruce Brooks (ed.): Frank Lloyd Wright Collected Writings Volume 1. Rizzoli, New York, 1992
▶ Pfeiffer, Bruce Brooks (ed.): Frank Lloyd Wright Collected Writings Volume 2. Rizzoli, New York, 1992
▶ Pfeiffer, Bruce Brooks (ed.): Frank Lloyd Wright Collected Writings Volume 3. Rizzoli, New York, 1993
▶ Pfeiffer, Bruce Brooks (ed.): Frank Lloyd Wright Collected Writings Volume 4. Rizzoli, New York, 1994
▶ Pfeiffer, Bruce Brooks (ed.): Frank Lloyd Wright Collected Writings Volume 5. Rizzoli, New York, 1995
▶ Riley, Terence & Peter Reed: Frank Lloyd Wright, Architect. Museum of Modern Art, New York, 1994
▶ Sergeant, John: Frank Lloyd Wright's Usonian Houses. Whitney Library of Design, New York, 1984
▶ Secrest, Meryle: Frank Lloyd Wright. Alfred A. Knopf, New York, 1992
▶ Storrer, William Allin: The Frank Lloyd Wright Companion. University Of Chicago Press, Chicago, 1993
▶ Sweeney, Robert: Wright in Hollywood, Visions of a New Architecture. Architectural History Foundation, New York, 1994
▶ Wright, Frank Lloyd: Ausgeführte Bauten und Entwürfe von Frank Lloyd Wright. Wasmuth Verlag, Tübingen, 1986 (reprint of 1910 portfolio edition)
▶ Wright, Frank Lloyd: An Autobiography. Barnes & Noble, New York, 1998